Privacy, PLEASE!

gaining independence from your parents

Privacy, PLEASE!

gaining independence from your parents

by Odile Amblard
illustrated by Céline Guyot
edited by Kate O'Dare

sunscreen

Library of Congress Cataloging-in-Publication Data
Amblard, Odile.
Privacy, please! : gaining independence from your parents /
by Odile Amblard ; illustrated by Celine Guyot.
p. cm. — (Sunscreen)
ISBN 978-0-8109-8357-1 (harry n. abrams, inc.)
1. Parent and teenager. 2. Autonomy in adolescence. I. Title.
HQ799.15.A52 2009
155.5'1825—dc22
2008033915

Text copyright © 2009 Odile Amblard
Illustrations © 2009 Céline Guyot

Translated by Natalie Kone

Book series design by Higashi Glaser Design

Printed and bound in China
10 9 8 7 6 5 4 3 2 1

Amulet Books are available at special discounts when purchased in quantity
for premiums and promotions as well as fundraising or educational use.
Special editions can also be created to specification. For details, contact
specialmarkets@hnabooks.com or the address below.

HNA ■■■■■
harry n. abrams, inc.
a subsidiary of La Martinière Groupe
115 West 18th Street
New York, NY 10011
www.hnabooks.com

contents

LEAVE ME ALONE.
I WANT TO BE
WITH MY FRIENDS.
DO NOT DISTURB.
I NEED SOME SPACE.
LEAVE ME ALONE.
I WANT TO BE
WITH MY FRIENDS.

Adolescence is stormy for everyone; that's just part of the deal. But how those thunderclaps and lightning bolts affect one family is different from how they affect another. No matter what, the way you and your parents communicate will be unique. As a teenager, you are creating a new identity for yourself and, as parents, they are creating new identities as well. All of you guys are learning new roles "on the job"; no wonder there can be some rumbles. You are growing up: your body is changing, your mind is expanding, and you want to test your limits. All of that is part of being a teenager. You've been a kid from the get-go; to become an adult requires learning and making mistakes as the new you emerges. You're going to push your parents and ask for space, but all the while you'll still need their dependable and reassuring presence in your life. The difficulty of striking that balance—which changes as you do—is a major cause of conflict.

The way to keep things from getting too cloudy is to keep a dialogue going. It won't always be pretty, but it needs to happen. This book will look at the different aspects of starting that dialogue and keeping it going, as well as give you insight into your own issues, and some of your parents', too.

MOM, DAD, LISTEN!

parents or strangers?

you don't understand!

YOU MAKE THEM FEEL WELL, OLD!

i'm not
a baby!

another
perspective

having a
dialogue

i'm not
a baby!

Growing up is exciting, which you know because you're in the midst of it! You are burning three thousand calories a day—all so your body can move from childhood to adulthood. Everything about you is transforming: your body, your mind, your perspective on life, and all your ideas. Your childhood skin doesn't fit like it used to; suddenly, you feel awkward and all the

changes leave your body and heart feeling exposed. You'll get used to your new body, but it takes some time. Consider yourself a work in progress.

Growing up is a lot of work. Think back a few years . . . not that long ago you were little and your parents were absolutely the best, the strongest, the most beautiful people in the world. You shared their tastes, went where they did, and followed the path they chose for you. For a child, parents represent the adult world and what it means to be an adult. You just assume you'll grow up to be like them, right?

you don't
understand!

Now everything has changed. Your parents might even say they don't recognize you anymore. OK, not really, but almost! Can you blame them? There are some major changes going on. Girls: your womanly body is taking shape, and getting used to it isn't always easy—too big here, too small there, hair, pimples, etc. Boys: you're anxiously scouting for some hair on your upper lip, fighting zits, and wishing you had the nerve to ask the doctor if the size of your penis is normal.

And then there are your parents . . . watching every development. They've seen this moment coming since the day you were born, but they still can't

ph1

believe it's happening so soon. Not only is the baby they raised rapidly maturing, but now that "baby" is also provoking a whole new set of worries and anxieties in them. Once you would run over to tell them every detail of what you were thinking, now you're often silent or moody. The jokes that used to make you laugh now get an irritated eye-roll. Put yourself in their place: you, your happiness, your safety, your development as a person have been their preoccupation your entire life. Now all that hard work is paying off, but they aren't ready to let go. They have to get used to a new you, a surprising, sometimes baffling you who no longer wants to be cuddled or protected—except, of course, when you do!

you make them feel,
well, OLD!

OK, maybe not elderly, but suddenly you are going through things your parents remember experiencing very clearly. Seeing you whispering on the phone or mooning around because of a crush can cause serious flashbacks to their own adolescence. The difference is that now they are the mother or father. They remember their first flirtations, their plans to conquer or shake up the world . . . and yet, here they are with a kid who is thinking the very same things they once did! But now they have to be the responsible ones, they have some wrinkles, and they tend to be set in their ways.

ph1

Remember when you were a kid and time seemed to pass sooooooooo slowly? Well, as you age, things speed up. Those of you who plan on majoring in philosophy should remember this: perceptions of "time" have nothing to do with the minutes marked on a clock. Even though an adult and a teenager share the same twenty-four-hour days, the way they experience them is totally different. The adult feels that there aren't enough hours in the day and is stressed about what must be left undone. The teenager, on the other (minute) hand, sits in a math class that seems to never end while feeling that the phone call he or she is waiting for will never, ever, in a million years come.

ieRRE

germaiNE

ROSE

LEON

JuLiette

another perspective

So much has changed. Here you are, girls, wearing lipstick and tight jeans. And boys, you're checking out your body in the mirror and maybe beginning to shave. All these physical changes are nothing compared with the tumult that's going on inside you, though. Your mind is changing, along with your dreams and attitude toward life. These mental changes can easily upset the equilibrium established between you and your parents. According to psychologists, one way that this commonly occurs is through a reactivation of the Oedipus complex.

The Oedipus complex? Yep, it's an inevitable stage of psychological development in humans. Around age three or four, small children unconsciously feel emotions toward their parents that are both hostile and loving. A little boy might proclaim, "When I'm older, I'm going to marry mommy," while a girl might act out at her mother while behaving affectionately with her father. All of this is completely normal. And you also start to learn that you will one day find someone other than your parents to love.

rivalry?

$\int$ince adolescence functions in many ways like a second birth, those long-forgotten feelings of hostility and love can surface without you being conscious of them. This might explain the tensions and frictions that suddenly emerge between you and your parents. For example, you might unconsciously see your mom as a rival, and she may feel a little competitive when confronted with you in your miniskirt. In the same vein, some moms have trouble with their son's first girlfriend, as they can't quite accept the idea that they are now not the only woman in their son's life.

parents or
strangers?

So things are tough for your parents? How should you know? And, furthermore, you have other things to think about, like yourself. But how much do you really know about them? Do you really look at them every day—your mom with her crazy schedule and your father who has trouble getting home before eight at night because work takes up so much time? You know technically what they do for work, but do you have any idea what they actually do all day? In what kind of environment? With what kind of boss and what sort of freedom or limitations? Another secret aspect of your parents' lives is

their relationship as a couple. And that's how it should be. Their private life is their business, and it doesn't concern you. In the end, what details you do know still add up to a pretty blurry image. That's normal, too. Just keep in mind that they have a life outside of being your parents. If they seem cranky, it might not be because of you at all but because of a bad day at work.

On the other hand, you might have talkative parents who want to share too much. Don't feel that you are obligated to listen to everything. Discussion is great, but burdening yourself with all of their worries is more than you have the capacity to deal with. Of course, pushing your mom away when

ph1

she has a ton to deal with isn't easy . . . but be sure to protest from time to time. You can't work out life's quandaries for yourself *and* your parents at the same time. At this moment in your life, you need parents who will stay in their roles—and you may need to remind them of that!

When it comes to the role of parents, everybody seems to agree on the job description. Raising you, educating you, guiding you, understanding you, having confidence in you, helping you, and then one that's so obvious sometimes you forget it: loving you. That may seem weird to you—"If they love me so much, why do they act this way?"—but the truth is that they are trying

ph1

their best. If one excellent, foolproof method for child rearing existed, you better believe that everybody would use it. But for better or worse, such a thing doesn't exist, so each attempt at raising a kid is unique. Want some proof? When you were born, your parents said to themselves that they would do better than their own parents. They were going to be less anxious, or pay more attention, be more loving or more disciplined. Now you've made it this far and nothing's certain. Did these new methods make you happier than they were at your age? Hard to tell. Were they better parents? Who knows! Why the confusion? Because, quite simply, the world is always changing.

no more
"because i said so!"

Attitudes toward authority have changed drastically over the past fifty years. Movements that began in the nineteenth century produced huge results in the twentieth: think of the civil rights movement and the women's liberation movement. Along with these groups, many others fought for recognition and rights. This has led to an acceptance of the view that in many cases there is no "right" or "wrong" way to be. People have different views and pursue different goals.

One of the main types of authority that was challenged was parental authority. Just being obedient, without thinking about why, was no longer considered the norm. Awesome, right? Yes, except this development introduces new things for both parent and child to deal with. One of the biggest changes is that it is now common for parents and their kids to talk more openly about what each wants.

having
a dialogue

Nowadays, parents are less likely to fall back on the old "because I said so," end of discussion that may have been necessary when you were younger. Now they attempt to see where you are coming from and understand things from your point of view. Notice the word "attempt"—this is often difficult for parents. They used to have to stop you from sticking forks

in electrical outlets, and now they are supposed to believe you have the maturity to go on a date or borrow the car? You can see the problem. This openness, though, means you have the opportunity as a younger person to check out other ways of life. You can see different options on TV, read about them, or maybe talk to a relative about their choices. There are a thousand different paths

ph1

to success, both personal and professional, and adolescence is when you begin considering seriously the ones that interest you—and weeding out the ones that don't. Something that worked beautifully for your parents might not be right for you, or vice versa! Take getting married. People say that marriage is the best way to raise a family, yet divorces are supercommon. You know plenty of kids who have happily divorced parents and others who have unhappily married ones. Then you might also know some loving, solid couples who aren't married at all. Life takes hard work and commitment, right? (Then why are get-rich-quick schemes so popular?) Your parents may have very definite views on life, marriage, and religion. Part of being a parent is the desire to instill in your children the values that are important to you. This is the time in your life when you'll look at the values your parents have given you and decide

ph1

which are staying with you into adulthood. Also, values that seem alien and oppressive may come to seem just right in a few years.

Violence, the economy, AIDS, war . . . the world can be pretty grim. All the time, you hear about rotten politicians and political parties, terrible job prospects, and people being hurt by those more powerful than they are. And you are supposed to get out there and be an adult? What helps you do that is conviction. Whom do you admire? Probably people who have overcome adversity to be the best at what they do. People who realized that complaining or hiding wouldn't make a difference—they had to get out there! They might be athletes or adventurers or eco-warriors, but you identify with their courage and commitment, their willingness to take risks and make sacrifices. In the meantime, while waiting to have as much punch as your heroes, you'll just relax and live at home a little longer. That's part of being young, right?

flying from
the nest

It used to be that people were out of the house at age eighteen—sometimes younger—and were considered adults. Today, you may legally be an adult at eighteen, but for most people adolescence easily stretches through college and into their mid-twenties. Many people choose to remain at home because they can save money or take a better job. The strange thing is that puberty is starting younger and younger, around ten or eleven for girls and twelve or thirteen for boys. This means that people are physically maturing earlier but staying at home even longer. It's a complex situation. And for many, spending more time living at home can mean more time to argue with your parents over the kind of lifestyle you would like to live.

KNOCK BEFORE ENTERING

no rest for
your parents

stay
out!

FRIENDS
OR
ENEMIES?

mom,
i'm hungry!

siblings

the secret
lives of
parents

mom,
i'm hungry!

Ah, Coke, pretzels, television: your reward for a hard day at school. It's well known that thinking can be hard on the brain. A salty snack and some really bad TV, however, are just what a brain needs after all that exertion. The more worthless the show, the more relaxing. Is it something truly stupid? Even better! You are a hard-working person and need to relax. After that relaxing interval, you'll head to your room for homework until you're called back out for dinner. Not bad! Except, two or three days a week you are expected to do things, things that do not involve TV or snacks. Things

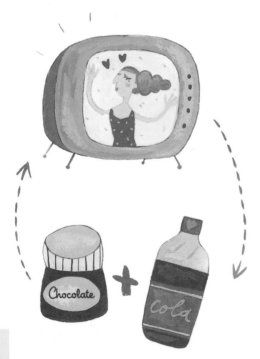

like vacuuming or setting the table or taking out the trash. Let's say you alternate doing these tasks with your little brother—you do even days, he does odd. On a good day, you get through your tasks almost whistling, but on a bad day you feel like the exploited victim of ungrateful parents. Have they no heart? And then

you pout, and sigh, and sulk . . . until you get a phone call from your friend
Meredith saying she'll pick you up for the game tomorrow. Suddenly, everything's cheerful again. You can't stop talking about the volleyball game and
your plans for total domination. Then the questions start: "By the way, Mom,
did you buy me Oreos and granola bars? You know I like them between games."
Followed by: "And you washed my uniform, right?" or: "And do you think my
bag will be dry? Are you sure?" Finishing up with a heated: "But Mom! You
knew that! My bag has to be ready tonight! Tomorrow, wake me up at eight!"

Such is the life of a superstar athlete, and you can bet your parents are having a ball with you.

Sometimes you're ecstatically happy; sometimes you're sullen. Some days you won't stop talking, and others you are evasive. Your parents are never sure what mood you'll be in. You'll look into the refrigerator and complain that nobody's been shopping, but when your dad asks you to go put a bottle in the recycling bin, you snap, "Yeah, who's gonna study for my algebra test, then?" OK, that's it, they've had enough, they can only take so much rudeness before they react. When this happens, you have two choices. The first is to keep your head down and wait for things to blow over; the other is to straighten up and get ready for rebellion. Why do your parents have to give you these lectures? You swear they give you pimples and go in one ear and out the other. The truth is that your parents have to do it. All the knowledge you acquired in childhood now needs to be reinforced and reaffirmed. They know that you are pushing and testing them, but even so it can be hard to keep cool.

no rest
for your parents

Are your parents happy to be parents? Sure, but they're also exhausted. You've perfected the art of a well-reasoned argument: "Why can't I watch TV after a certain hour, but I can read as late as I want?" "You want me to be generous, but you won't let me give my comics collection away. Why?" Be careful, though, because what seems like a reasonable question to you may strike them as a huge rejection. If you come home and announce that you no longer eat meat, for instance, they might feel that you are striking out against them and the hard work they do to keep you well fed. They may

ph2

feel that you are rejecting willy-nilly everything that is important to them. On the other hand, they may feel impressed—and a little worried—about your ability to try out new ideas and make effective arguments. They listen to how passionately you can argue, and it makes them proud. They just want to make sure you are solid before you start shaking up everything around you.

contention
in the air

It's too bad your parents don't always have the time or patience to listen to you when you suddenly have the itch to talk. Between the Internet, the news, and what you are reading in school, you are quickly becoming a font of information. You certainly have access to more than your parents did at the same age. As you take in all this new information, you may form views that are different from your parents'. This can—as you probably know!—lead to arguments. The thing is, each argument serves a purpose. Both you and your parents are learning about one another and your new roles. When you ask your parents to justify their positions, they can make their ideas clearer to you while seeing that you are no longer a baby who accepts whatever he or she is told. Although things might get heated, eventually these discussions will allow you to have better communication as adults—as long as both sides try to keep an open mind!

stay out!

But in your own room, you reign supreme. Hey, watch it! That pizza box is on the floor for a reason! You've been taught how to behave in the house—don't make a mess in the living room, knock before opening your parents' door— but now the time has come to talk to your parents about how you'd like your room treated. This is best accomplished by explaining that you need to have your space and privacy respected. Shouting a shrilly "Get out!" when they try to open the door will not work as well. Being able to go to your room and shut the door gives

you a chance to have a separate space where you can collect your thoughts, plan, and dream without being watched. It isn't that you have something to hide or intend to do bad stuff—you just want to be able to listen to music or stare at the wall without explaining what you are doing. If you share a room, you probably have a drawer or a box that you can lock to protect things you don't want to share.

Even the most understanding parent in the world won't be able to resist poking in occasionally and demanding that your pigsty be cleaned up. The severity of the threat depends on the family. You might get away with shoving everything in the closet once a week, or you may need to commit to tidying up to keep the peace.

ph2

are you STILL
in the bathroom!?

Mirror, mirror on the wall . . . Aside from your room, your other favorite spot in the house may be the bathroom. You want to observe the changes you are going through, and the bathroom mirror is a silent, trustworthy ally that won't go telling everyone in the world you worry about the amount of armpit hair you have. Your parents probably remember the hours they spent staring at themselves and will leave you alone. However, other

people do have a genuine right—and need—to use the bathroom, so think about getting in your bathroom-time at off-hours. Before work and school might cause a huge traffic jam! Sometimes parents will discreetly slip something in that they think you might need but don't want to ask for: Clearasil, depilatory cream, razors, tampons, maybe even a box of condoms. Before you start to fume about your parents being nosy, think about this as a way for them to acknowledge what is going on and signal that they are there if you need them. Just like you, parents don't always do the best job of saying what they mean. Sometimes they feel foolish or clumsy . . . it isn't easy for parents to be present without being omnipresent!

siblings

Whether it's drab or crazy, thorny or rosy, family life is a crash course in being a person. It is where you grow, cry, laugh, and learn to share and take responsibility. Your comrades in all of it are your brothers and sisters. When you were tiny, you learned to "share" your parents with them. You may have shared a room, and you've certainly shared toys, clothes, and outings.

Maybe you've known kids who were only children and didn't share at all. Believe it or not, they probably dreamed of having someone to ride bikes with or play video games with. If you have younger siblings, you may resent that they want you to stay a child with them: you have to play with them and watch them. On the other hand, you get to be older and wiser, teaching them slang and showing them your latest model jet or skateboard. And on days when you're feeling good, you're proud to be in charge of the younger ones all afternoon. But if it means canceling plans with friends, watch out. Suddenly they are ruining your life!

friends or enemies?

In your impatience to grow up you may feel caught between two ages. It's always Emily who sits on Mom's lap and Elise who usually gets a bedtime story. You feel too old for all that but miss the attention. Meanwhile, Jessica, at seventeen, gets permission to stay out until midnight on Saturdays, while you, at fourteen, are told you're too young. Oh, really? You're old enough to hear all her secrets and listen to her music!

All of this "in-between" stuff can cause tension between siblings, but it also gives you strength. Together you form a whole unit. Working together,

you educate your parents about what each of you needs. The oldest is the forerunner, fighting for rights and liberty. The younger ones are envious but get the benefits of all of the older sibling's hard work. Sometimes you can't stand each other and sometimes you fight, but you always make up. That's life in a family.

the secret lives
of parents

Yes, believe it or not, your parents exist as people, not just as your parents. They have friends, professional concerns, and sometimes personal problems. You probably aren't aware of them, and that's perfectly fine. However, sometimes the tensions mount and you see your parents fight. It's scary, and it might leave you wondering if they are going to divorce. The thing to remember is that people can be in love with a capital *L* and not agree on everything. Furthermore, seeing how people—even your parents—handle conflict and tension is a great way for you to see what works and what just seems to lead to more arguing.

Occasionally, an event in your parents' lives becomes a major event in the life of the whole family. If your parents are separated or divorced, you already know this. When such a large upheaval takes place, you need to remember that you cannot fix things or make them go back to the way they were. The best thing to do is let your parents know you love them and you'll do your best to try to understand what is going on. What you shouldn't do is become a shoulder for your parents to cry on. They're adults who have chosen their own paths; you are still developing and not ready for that job.

parental authority

A major part of being parents—despite their children's ability to sway them—is staying on course, whether you like it or not! At home, parents make the decisions because it is their home. A family is never a true democracy: not every member has an equal vote. Your vote may count toward what to have for dessert or what color to

Chad

Melissa

paint the kitchen, but it won't mean as much when discussing your future. In many respects, your parents are responsible for you. They need to show you that, as important as you are to them, the whole world doesn't revolve around you. Nor do they want you to make the mistake of thinking the world can be molded to suit you. Whatever protection and guidance they give now is offered with an eye toward a future rough patch that they might not be able to help with. All of this is done because parents have a job other than making sure you make it to adulthood in one piece. They need to prepare you to live—and thrive—in society. How do they do it? Well, first by transmitting to you a sense of identity and cultural heritage: this is who we are, and this is what we believe in. So in between telling you to clean your room and do your homework, your parents are showing you what it means to live in a complex society where compromise, tolerance, and diplomacy are key skills.

Maria

some real letters

about parents

"When your parents are too nice or lenient, it's easy to do whatever you want but you feel strange. Its like, how do you know what's good or bad? If your parents never say anything, it feels like they don't care or are just too busy to notice. But if you have parents who are too strict, then it's like you just want to get away all the time. If they are super-tough, you end up afraid. If they are really controlling then you become obsessed with getting out and having fun."

—Susan

"Whether they are authoritarian or gentle, mean, nice, or whatever, they are still my parents. Even when they annoy me to death, I still think about them and wonder what they would think of what I'm doing."

—Scott

"Parents want to stop their kids from making the same mistakes they did, but they can't. Each person has to experience life for themselves."

—Maggie

"Parents want to put their kids in a mold so they come out exactly like they want. It doesn't work—everyone has their own personality."

—Howard

SCHOOL'S IN SESSION

the
questions

10 ÷ 3
12 + 14 ↑
× 4210.
↘ 8 + 12

i don't know
what i want

CAN ANYONE
HEAR ME?

when the
future feels a
long way off

college

**too much
pressure!**

do cool
parents
exist?

middle school and high school:
your world

As you get older, school gets more and more impor-

tant. Your class load is heavier and more diverse. But school

isn't just about academic work; it's also where most of your

personal life takes place. You have friends, maybe even a best friend

there. And you learn a lot outside of the classroom:

talking in the hallways, the relationships you've

developed with teachers, working on disciplining

yourself. It's also where you make mistakes, some bigger

than others: disrupting class, copying a friend's assignment, or get-

ting involved in tricky emotional situations.

not your
parents' world

School is most of your world. By definition, your parents are excluded. When you were a kid, you'd come home and talk to them all about it. Now you say less and less. You're figuring out things for yourself. You might tell a story or ask your parents for some input on an essay, but you don't reveal everything—like how nervous you are about the calculus exam, or the wonderful moments you spent with Alex on the field trip to the Museum of Modern Art, or card games in study hall. These small details are yours. Keeping some things private is a good idea. Everyone needs to cultivate his or her own interior garden.

the
questions

"How was your day?" "What'd you do after school?" "How'd you do on the test?" Sometimes your parents' questions can feel like pestering. Do you constantly ask if they worked hard at the office? It's better if you don't, because in all honesty, your school life and their work life have very little in common. Furthermore, as parents, they have an obligation to make sure you are educated, not just because they love you—but also because they are legally obligated to make sure you remain in school until a certain age.

But the law isn't why your parents want you to do well in school. They feel that your middle school and high school years are going to have an effect on your future and the opportunities open to you. As the months pass, your parents get more concerned—so now do you understand all those questions? They want you to be successful and to participate, not be a tourist just passing through your education!

they are
CRAZY
about grades

Imagine the situation: you're tight-lipped about how you're feeling, and your parents are concerned. What's the one concrete way they can tell how you're doing? Grades! "That's all you care about!" you complain. And it isn't fun for anyone when your parents need to sign report cards that are, well, mediocre.

You do have a point, though. Grades are a small part of your schooling. They provide a marker that can show where you are excelling or could use more improvement. There are a million different ways to get a C. Did you not study? Did you make a bunch of careless mistakes so that your grade suffered? Or was your last grade a D and now things are looking up? OK, so grades mean different things, but parents only have so many ways to engage with your schoolwork. If you don't talk to them, or if they left school early and have difficulty understanding your work, your grades are going to be what they are looking at!

The strange thing is that while your parents tell you to be more concerned with grades, your teachers might be complaining that you focus too much on grades. So how to deal? Don't feel that you must rebel against the grade system to make a point. Doing well will make things easier for you—both now and in the future.

do cool
parents exist?

Yours, you've decided, are fundamentally not cool—especially when it comes to schoolwork. You try to relax in front of the TV and they want to know if you've finished your homework. When you attempt to tell them how boring some classes are, they tell you that the classes will be useful one day. One day! Hah! It seems like your parents don't understand at all.

At your age you want to live immediately and intensely. Exactly the opposite attitude to the one that school demands. You want to get out there and shake things up, so it isn't surprising that you may clash with parents and teachers—the people who maintain order.

Your schooling is also a learning process for your parents. They learn that they can't control all the choices you make and that you may have interests that aren't what they had in mind for you. They also can't study for you or take exams in your place, so they need to get used to having less control. They want to push you to succeed; the question is: how far and for how long?

too much

pressure!

The older you get, the more pressure you'll face in school. The largest source of conflict between teenagers and their parents is school and academic performance. Parents want you to do well in school and on your SATs so that you can get into a good college and maybe even receive a scholarship. They feel that this will make finding a job easier and help you achieve a stable life as a young adult. But relentless pressure to do well doesn't make your life any easier. In an attempt to keep you motivated, they may threaten, "One more C and you're quitting dance!" or bribe you with "All A's and I'll buy you a car." Both scenarios put more pressure on you. Maybe extra pressure works, though, and you find that the cracking of the whip makes you do better. If the opposite is true, and the more they push the more you slump, talk to them immediately. If that doesn't work, go to another adult, maybe a teacher or a trusted relative, for help finding ways to broach the subject so that your parents understand the problem.

i'm going
crazy!

Sometimes parents set the bar too high and you feel like you'll lose your mind. There are all sorts of reasons for this: maybe they regret not doing better in school and want to fix the mistake with you. The problem is, people don't work that way! You have your own strengths and weaknesses and can't fix the past for your parents. Maybe your older sister was brilliant at math, so they expect the same from you. Same problem—you and your sister are different people. The ideal way to deal with this problem is by talking to them about it. Go for it—express how you feel. What if you end up screaming at each other? It might happen, but you might also get some insight into each other that can help. They want you to quit volleyball because of your math grade? Argue! Tell them how much the sport means to you, what an important part of your life it is, and how happy it makes you. Losing it would make you feel completely stifled. But that doesn't mean you can use volleyball practice to excuse yourself from a bad grade or missed class.

can anyone
hear me?

𝒟𝑜 𝑦𝑜𝑢𝑟 𝑝𝑎𝑟𝑒𝑛𝑡𝑠 𝑙𝑜𝑜𝑘 at you like you speak another language when you talk about school? Get that friendly teacher or relative involved as a mediator.

But what if things are worse than that—it isn't just your grades but your whole life that feels like one confusing mess? There are people to talk to, like school nurses, psychologists, and guidance counselors. Your doctor—even a pediatrician—can provide advice or suggest someone to talk to. If things feel unbearable, speak up!

when the future feels
a long way off

One way to cope with what feels like an interminable wait is to break up your time into smaller pieces and give yourself specific goals. Aim to finish reading a novel by the end of the month, get your English grade up by the end of the semester, and raise your speed in swim practice. All of these are things you can plan now rather than worrying about in the future. A nice benefit of working this way is that your parents will see that you are responsible and able to get things done. That means they'll be more likely to trust your judgment.

i don't know
what i want

How do you figure out what you want? Well, by what you are doing right now: talking to friends and teachers, reading, and seeing movies. All of these activities contribute to the formation of your tastes and interests. You may already feel a certain way about the importance of money, whether or not you'd like to travel, or if you must have a job that involves music or fashion or sports.

One way to keep all these ideas together is to jot them down in a notebook. Talk to the people you admire about why they do the work they do and what led them to it. Do you want to work alone or in a group? Outside or inside? Should your job be manual or intellectual labor? What kind of education do you need to do the job?

You have years to decide exactly what will make you happy, so give yourself the space to learn about all different types of occupations and pursuits, and remember, it's never too late to be a success.

letter from
a mother
to her son

My dearest little one,
Darn, I'm not quite used to how old you are. I'll try
again.

My almost grown son,
You're sulking in your room right now and I don't
want to bother you, so I'm writing a letter. I'm not
going to show it to you, but I want to put these ideas
down on paper.

This morning you came back from your camping trip looking exhausted and dragging your huge bag. You wouldn't answer questions with more than a yes or no, so I let it drop. Why are you in such a bad mood? Do you even know why?

I miss you, and it makes me lonely. When I was your age, I had a diary where I wrote all the things my mother did to make me hate her. I swore that when I had kids I would remember that a fifteen-year-old isn't a child and needs to be treated with respect. And now, here we both are. I'm an adult, you're fifteen, and

I feel totally powerless. I miss my sweet kid. How warm and snuggly you were when you'd sit on my lap. Now in his place I have an alien who wants nothing to do with me but inhabits the same house. It's true you occasionally speak up: "Are we out of Coke?" or "When's dinner?" or "Gross, beans again? I hate beans, you know that!" And I guess you are affectionate, especially when you want something: "Hey, Mom? Could Jim sleep over tonight?" or "Don't you owe me my allowance?"

When you do speak to me I can't always understand, despite thinking my grasp of slang is pretty good. "Peace out?" What?

I know better than to disturb the sacred sanctuary of your bedroom, but you have no problem raiding my office. Any idea what happened to that box of pens I bought? I don't really get why you're so angry at me. Yes, I've committed some unpardonable sins: your last sneakers weren't Nikes, and I told your friend Philip he should say hello when he calls. . . .

Sometimes I feel really discouraged. I tell myself that I must have failed somehow in raising you.

But sometimes I can still see the love in your eyes, and it repairs my confidence and perks me up. And this letter will make both of us laugh when I give it to you in thirty years and you have a fifteen-year-old of your own!

Love,
   Mom

LEAVE ME MY

SNEAKERS

experience

conflict,
that's life!

rules!
what rules

allowance, please

going out

talking is the solution!

allowance,
please

Considering what a consumption-driven society we live in, the desire to have some money of your own isn't crazy. As you spend more time away from mom and dad, you want money to "invest" as you see fit. Herein lies the benefit of having an allowance—but also the problem for lots of parents. First, controlling the budget means, in a sense, controlling you. If they won't give you money for a movie, then you aren't going and that's that. But if you have an allowance, you have more freedom to decide what you want to do. Parents also fear that you'll spend the money they worked so hard to earn in a silly way. Should they have to fork over thirty dollars so you can buy music they find painful to listen to? Another concern your parents might have is that you don't understand the value of money. Saying no to an allowance is a way for parents to get you to think about the dangers of a world where *having* is more important than *being*. They want you to analyze why you want things before you buy them: Is it advertising? Your friends? Or is it really your style?

When confronted with this reasonable attitude, you need to be reasonable, too. There are plenty of arguments in your favor; you just need to make them convincingly. Maybe your parents have forgotten what a drag it was to

ask for money every time they wanted to go out. Or maybe they didn't feel they needed cash when they were your age, but surely they agree that times have changed? Have you really explained why

you need a regular amount of money that you can spend or save? They might not find the answer "to be like my friends" convincing, but it is true. They know you spend all your time together, and if you don't have the money to go to the movies or the ice-skating rink, you'll be at home brooding in your room. Ah, cruel fate!

i need to learn to
manage a budget

Are they convinced yet? They might tell you that the family budget is too tight for something extra like an allowance. Since you aren't a huge egomaniac, you should be able to understand this problem. You could suggest that you be allowed to manage a small amount for yourself that would have gone toward your clothes or other expenses. You can explain that it will teach you to manage money responsibly. Also, once they give you the money, that's

it—no surprise requests if something comes up and you've already spent your allowance. Part of managing a budget is planning, and unless you are good at it, you may find you are out of funds long before your next installment gets paid. Are you sure you still want an allowance?

cars:
a taste of freedom

Having a little bit of cash and access to a car means one thing: freedom! You need to be out and about, doing what you please when you please. Want to see a concert in the next town? You can go! It's a dream come true for you but often an absolute nightmare for your parents.

Why? They remember being teenagers. The aimless driving, the distractions, the showing off. That's why they want you to be extracareful. Speeding? You promise, you swear, you cross your heart, you won't go over the speed limit! Traffic laws? You promise, you swear, you cross your heart, you'll follow every single one! So why are there so many accidents?

Of course, accidents only happen to other people. . . . They could never happen to you. That's exactly the attitude your parents fear most. They know that to live without taking risks isn't living. But there are risks and then there are RISKS. Between you and your parents, that's what the debate is about. They know very well that during adolescence, you crave liberty and independence. You need to prove yourself, to take some risks. But they wouldn't want your independence to cost you . . . too much. So sometimes the answer is no. No to your own car at sixteen. Yes, maybe, at eighteen after some serious Drivers Ed. No to driving alone, but yes to driving accompanied by Mom. Maybe your parents are hoping that you won't be crafty and hard working enough to be able to buy your own car! Are they fighting the inevitable? Absolutely—but they just want you to be safe.

going out

With or without a car, you need to get out of the house. Not that your parents are such a huge drag but because you just feel good when you're out. Seeing your friends or a boyfriend or girlfriend without your parents observing can be wonderfully relaxing. For a few hours you don't have to report to anyone or explain anything. You can speak to your friends honestly, using the language that you want—no worries about being over-heard. It's so different from life at home that sometimes you wish you could stop time and things would stay just like this. Then you have to wait a whole week to meet again. When the weekend comes, there you are again, back together. At first, just hanging out seems like the best thing ever, but then . . . a party.

You'll probably talk about it for weeks in advance—what to wear, who'll be invited, what to bring. It's going to be fabulous. Sean will be there, and Jen's friend, lots of people from school, good music, maybe even cigarettes and alcohol, which are strictly forbidden at home. Everybody will be there . . . except me? Um, no way. That's impossible! I've been waiting for this forever. Not being able to go makes you feel miserable, but even that won't stop your best friends from going and talking about it all next week. There'll be other times, so for now just savor the fun you have had and be patient.

The more you grow up, the more you want to go out and the more reasons—both good and bad—your parents have to worry. As long as you are at home, they know you're safe. It's as if you are more at risk of breaking your arm with Becca at the ice-skating rink than in-line skating in the driveway. Parents worry—that's what they do. They worry, and they have powerful imaginations that can conjure up all sorts of terrible things. They often can't help but imagine the worst: an accident, an argument that turns violent, a silly risk. They doubt you, and they doubt themselves for letting you out of their sight. But it isn't like they haven't warned you!

Not only are they worried, but they're also responsible. Even on the street, you're still their child. Their role as your parents doesn't end when you leave the house, and they want to be sure that you aren't behaving like a maniac when you go out. Right or wrong, they aren't sure you have the maturity to evaluate all the risks that you face. And why should they? They're in no hurry for you to grow up—it's just you who's in a rush. They know that every step is leading up to the day when you leave home for good.

ph4

So they want to establish some safeguards. They hold you accountable, and they watch your behavior both up close and from afar. They give you limits to make sure you can respect them. They ask you to be home by 11:30, not only because they don't want to spend all night worried sick— but because they also want to make sure that they can trust you. And 11:30 means 11:30. They want to know whose house you are at, both to make sure you are safe and to know that you're telling the truth. If they catch you in a lie, not only will they be disappointed, but they'll also establish all sorts of new rules and methods for verifying what you tell them. They don't want you to feel that anything goes or that what you tell them has no meaning.

For some people your age, telephoning to tell your mom where you are is absolutely no big deal. Others detest it. They feel that if they are allowed to go out and it's before their curfew, why should they have to report in? They aren't babies; why should they have to negotiate all the time to go to a party, or stay out late, or borrow the car?

OK, you aren't a baby. That much is apparent to the naked eye. But what's the big deal about earning some of the trust you demand from your parents? How do you do it? Simple: start at the beginning. Your parents are worried about an upcoming party. Have the host over so they can meet him or her and

see that he or she is a normal kid. Are they worried that parties will distract from schoolwork? Work Friday night and Saturday afternoon so you are finished in time for the party Saturday night. Want your parents to have more confidence in you? Accept a curfew and abide by it all the time. They don't want Lucas driving you home? Let your dad come get you. Too embarrassing? "Meet me on the sidewalk at midnight, OK, Dad?" He won't mind.

Still not happy? Some of your friends come and go exactly when they please. They can even sleep over at parties. There are as many different kinds of families as there are ways of raising kids, and parents have different mindsets. Ask yourself: Who has more fun going out? Sarah, who does it all the time, or you, for whom it feels special? Who feels best at the end of the night? You, for making it home by curfew and fulfilling your obligation, or Sarah, who has no one waiting for her?

experience

As much as you may feel good in your own skin, and have a satisfying relationship with your parents, you can't stop yourself from . . . experimenting—out of curiosity or to feel like you're really living. Experiencing strong emotions—scaring yourself (a little or a lot), being passionate, having fun, pushing yourself, competing—provides some opportunities to find your limits and to experience a lot. But that isn't always enough . . .

When you leave childhood to head toward adulthood, you have a need to figure out what you're capable of, perhaps by proving to yourself that you are someone by mocking everything, including, above all, laws. You might steal CDs, tamper with your car, show off while driving, leave without paying for your coffee . . . stupid things. But why do you feel the need to shock others, or to frighten your parents so that they continue to worry about you? Unless you find balance, you could wander down a dangerous road.

rules! what rules?

From one small thrill to the next, you always dream of going further—verging on the forbidden. It's kind of fun to scare yourself. With friends you talk about all the things you could be doing. Cigarettes, alcohol, pot—what good does getting high do you? You talk about it among yourselves. What are the pros and cons? The pros advocate that it's an element of party-ing, that it's good to really have fun, to forget everything, and to know what it's like to get stoned. The cons argue: yes to experiences, yes to great par-ties, no to stupid drinking competitions that lead nowhere—except, some-times, the hospital.

There again, you and your parents have to find a balance. Short of for-bidding you from ever going out, it's impossible to prevent you from having experiences. But it's also impossible for them not to worry: And if something went wrong? And if you let yourself be influenced by your friends? Their arguments swing between their concern for your safety and the necessity that you respect the law and yourself.

conflict,
that's life!

You want to celebrate the end of the semester at Emma's house. Your parents feel that at thirteen you're too young. So you are angry and bitter. Shut up in your room, you fall apart—a few kicks to the furniture and then you flop on the bed in an outburst of tears. Why? Why? Why? Why are they so old-fashioned? Can't they understand you need to have fun? You're outraged, furious, and then . . . it passes. You feel guilty for having lost your temper with them. They feel bad for putting you in such a state. Don't worry. These fights aren't dangerous for any of you. In fact, they're healthy: better some furniture kicking than silence or indifference.

talking is
the solution!

The only problem is that, as voices get raised, tension rises, too. That means it gets harder for you to actually hear what the other person is saying. Emotion takes over. Try to take a breather and return to the argument when everyone is calmer. Are they afraid you'll start partying all the time? That your younger brothers will want to go out, too? Do they not have the financial resources to support your nights out? Rather than fire back at them, take some time to think over what they said. You might even try responding in letter form. If it doesn't convince them, at least you were able to express yourself.

Today it feels like your parents are stifling you, but at least they are watching out for and protecting you. You may not agree, but they always have an answer. All the constraints may weigh on you, but they ultimately make you stronger. You oppose your parents, but that conflict is part of forging a character of your own, and they know that. Plus, think how much fun it will be to go out when you finally can!

The best thing you can do is keep the communication lines open. As long as there is a dialogue with your parents, hopefully you can find a compromise, or at least rest assured knowing that you were able to express yourself.

IT'S MY LIFE

friends take center stage

Chad

Me

it doesn't concern you!

YOU CAN'T UNDERSTAND

no
comments!

open
house

speak
up

my way

Unique or looking to fit in, your personality can camouflage itself, depending on your mood. Do you hide your eyes behind a curtain of hair or go for a uniform of baggy jeans and sweatshirts, and unlaced Converse? Everybody has a look. Like a real second skin, your clothes both conceal and reveal you. At school, separate cliques might have distinct looks and everyone recognizes their symbols. Not everyone has the resources—financial, mainly—to outfit themselves exactly as they'd like, and this may lead to some scheming and arguments at home. The scheme might involve asking Grandma or your uncle to get you something your parents don't want to spend money on. Then arguments start because the beautiful dress your mom picked out for you hangs unloved in your closet while

you wear the same worn-out jeans every day. Eventually you work out a system: Mom comes with you to the stores but promises to let you choose; your monthly budget includes a sum of money for your clothes. Finally you give up without a fight because, between presents, sales, and purchases from catalogs, you've constructed yourself a look worthy of your ambitions!

How you look is your business, right? Usually parents agree. They prefer to save their energy for more important battles like schoolwork or going out. They understand that the "disguise" you've adopted is a means of expression and sometimes a way to provoke them. Especially when you choose a look that's in strong opposition to their style! Some things just won't fly: "That? No! Not as long as you live in this house!" In this case, it's useless to keep fighting. The limits are clearly defined. If you disobey them, it's your neck. If you refuse to back down, your parents will only be able to react more firmly. Otherwise, they'd be sending the message that they don't mean what they say. All things considered, that would probably make you nervous!

Concerning music, your beloved music, the struggle is pretty similar. As much as your parents let you listen to and buy (with your money) what you want, they also refuse to let you make the whole house enjoy it! Your freedom stops where other people's freedom begins. As much as your parents understand that the "noise" that fills your room serves as a protective bubble, they neither want to endure your taste nor pay a fine because the neighbors keep calling the cops! And if you really want to educate them about your musical choices, lend them your iPod!

ph5

i'm the one who chooses
my friends

Friends are sacred. They're untouchable—even more so than your wardrobe or your music. The more you grow up, the larger the role they assume. While your parents sometimes seem to have difficulty keeping up with you, friends always maintain the right tempo. Naturally, they move like you. They understand you; they don't judge you as your parents do. They listen to you without always wanting to give you advice as your parents do. And when they get ahead of you, they share their experiences without lecturing you.

no comments!

It's true—during adolescence having friends is key. They allow you to distance yourself little by little from the family cocoon and to find outside sources of affection and warmth. Different from you, they help you discover new ways of thinking. But they're similar enough that it's reassuring. You're all going through the same things, you feel the same emotions, share the same fears and the same joys. With them, you create your first personal relationships, without your parents as buffers.

That's why you don't necessarily have the desire to bring your friends around all the time. You prefer to keep them a bit secret: it's your personal life; it doesn't concern your parents. And then, your parents eventually meet them, when they ring the doorbell, grab a snack in the kitchen, or camp out in your bedroom. Occasionally, you even let them talk a bit! What's unbearable, though, are the little judgments: "Oh, he seems like a nice boy." "Do you hear how she talks? How can you be friends with her?" Little comments like that hurt a lot. What right do your parents have to question your choices? How can they judge without knowing? Of course, you can make a mistake, even trust someone who doesn't deserve it. But you need to learn! Your mistakes, even painful ones, will help you distinguish "good" friends from "bad" ones.

ph5

friends take
center stage

𝓕𝓸𝓻 𝓹𝓪𝓻𝓮𝓷𝓽𝓼, the importance placed on friends is often an unmistakable sign. If they feel they've been pushed to the side, adolescence has officially begun.

Little by little, parents realize that they're no longer the center of your emotional life. You ask to go out more and more, you're influenced by a new force coming from elsewhere: from the outside. For parents, seeing their kid be willing to open himself or herself up to others, and be capable of cultivating his or her own relationships, is a source of real satisfaction. They know they've done a good job.

This satisfaction is often coupled with a little heartache (if not, life would be too simple!). How much depends on your parents, and on the intensity of their relationship with you and on the richness of their own personal lives. The heartache is natural: you prefer your friends to your parents. You ask less and less for their advice, their opinions. Your final departure from the nest suddenly feels very close. . . . Without a doubt, they don't go so far as to consider your friends rivals, but they would like to be a little reassured, to be reminded that you love them. As much as your parents keep saying "that's life" and think these changes are all very normal, they still have nostalgia for all those hugs, kisses, and smiles you gave them when you were a kid!

open house

The best way to reassure them (if you want to) is to bring friends
to the house. At least Mom will get a glimpse of them and get to talk to them
for three minutes. Most often, this will be enough to appease your parents
and help them easily accept the fact that you'll be spending your afternoons
in one of your friends' homes. Especially if Mom has their telephone numbers!
Her biggest joy as well is for you to invite Laura to spend the night at your
house. Of course, it creates a bit of a disturbance! Your mother has to put a
mattress on the floor and tolerate the uncontrollable laughter and gossip-
ing until the wee hours of the morning in your bedroom. . . . But you're there,
which makes her happy! It's also the best compliment: you aren't ashamed of
your parents, and you must be happy at home since you're willing to hang out
with your best friend there!

still, you'd
rather be out

Everything becomes complicated when you refuse to allow your personal life to mingle with your family life. You always manage to get invited somewhere else. Your parents are allowed to pick up when the phone rings on the express condition that they don't try to find out who is on the other end of the line! If they dare ask you what Max's parents do, you fire back: "I don't judge people on their parents' jobs!" Why so touchy? You simply don't want to mix your life with their lives!

it doesn't
concern you!

You talk about your friends grudgingly. You recount an anecdote to show that Flora's parents are "cool." If you ask your parents, "John's nice, don't you think?" you're only looking for agreement. . . . In a pinch, you let yourself be comforted if you're a bit disappointed by Erin. But you hate being asked questions! Even nicely. In your eyes, it's not friendly interest—it's an inquisition! For most teens, nothing is holier than the law of silence! It's top secret. You despise all of the little family remarks: "Hey, was that Chloe waiting for you on the street corner?" or "Wow! Somebody's dressed up!" or even, "Here, a letter for you!" Why are they always prying? As annoying as it may be, your parents just want to be a part of your life. And remember, you do have control over how much information you share with them about your friends. But, cut them some slack, they just want to know you're OK.

you can't
understand

You push your parents to the edge of your personal life. They can try to understand, but in reality, they'll never really succeed. How could they put themselves in your place? They don't feel the same way about life that you do. The times are different, the relationships between girls and guys are different, the desires and the dangers are different. And then, parents always look at things from their responsible and worried perspective.

To get the lowdown and advice, you go first to your very close friends. They experience the same setbacks, share the same emotions. For more personal or more specific questions, magazines, books, or sometimes the school nurse or a doctor will always be there. That's enough for you! You feel like you're "well equipped," maybe even saturated with information! All you're lacking is personal experience. And no one can give you that!

needing help . . .

Nor will anyone be able to stop you from having the blues or experiencing sadness every now and then. Even true friends hesitate to intervene when you're upset, but they know how to be quiet at your side and show support. That's exactly what you ask from your parents: to reassure you with their presence, and most of all not to label anything a good life lesson. Little things, OK, but, "it wasn't right for you" or "you'll see, it'll pass," no, not helpful!

speak up

Taboos are gone. In your home and in the media, everything is talked about. Or almost everything. Information circulates. Ideas have evolved. This simplifies your life. But not your parents'! How to keep guiding you without preaching? How to explain to you that love (like friendship) develops and shouldn't be rushed? How to tell you without freaking you out that only you will know when you are ready to have sex?

Parents have the right to protect you. As a result, they live with an impossible dilemma: they want to keep you informed without scaring you. They want to push you to think without playing the stodgy "guardians of morality." They warn you not to act too quickly but don't want to force you back into childhood.

In any case, short of banging their fists on the table, they must let you know what they think: Yes, they think that girlfriends will distract you from your schoolwork; yes, they think that this girl is a bad friend; no, they don't want you to have sex right now. For that matter, if they didn't say anything, you'd be angry at them for not being concerned about you!

Being parents means making their feelings and opinions heard. They're just as legitimate as your own. Having stable, true-blue parents at your side can be helpful! Right?

by way of
conclusion

Observing the world with a more critical eye, distancing yourself, creating a top-secret private life—adolescence is a change! And a really strange and tiring time. Sure, it's fascinating and thrilling, but it can create a feeling of emotional overload. For you—and for your parents! Through all of it, you need to feel supported. Friends and best friends are made for the job. But you can also find solid allies in the adult camp! Look to people who are older than you and have some experiences to pass on to you, without being occupied with your parents' responsibilities and concerns for your education. They are more impartial but can give you the more mature perspective you need.

It can be an uncle, an aunt, an older cousin, even a guidance counselor. It's so fulfilling to feel like you're being listened to, recognized in your tastes, your anxieties, your dreams, by someone a little bit older than you. Since they're younger than your parents, you know that they'll really understand you. And above all, they represent good proof that there are numerous paths to becoming an adult! They pull you forward into adulthood and show you what's possible.

You so much need to be loved and accepted when you're an adolescent— that is never something to be embarrassed about! All the encouragement in

ph5

the world isn't too much, and it isn't a weakness to need it. This is tough stuff: A world in which you are neither completely a child nor an adult. A world in which you very much need your parents, if only to learn to separate yourself from them. A little. A lot. Abruptly. Tenderly. All of it depends on them and on you. And it's thanks to all of these relationships and all of these experiences that you will know how to live without them. Later on.

suggestions for further reading

Books

American Medical Association. *Girl's Guide to Becoming a Teen* (John Wiley & Sons, Inc., 2006).

American Medical Association. *Boy's Guide to Becoming a Teen* (John Wiley & Sons, Inc., 2006).

Carlson, Richard. *Don't Sweat the Small Stuff for Teens: Simple Ways to Keep Your Cool in Stressful Times* (Hyperion, 2000).

David, Ken. *How to Live with Your Parents Without Losing Your Mind* (Zondervan, 1988).

Espeland, Pamela. *Life Lists for Teens: Tips, Steps, Hints, and How-Tos for Growing Up, Getting Along, Learning, and Having Fun* (Free Spirit Publishing, 2003).

McGraw, Jay. *Closing the Gap: A Strategy for Bringing Parents and Teens Together* (Simon & Schuster, 2001).

Potash, Marlin S., Laura Potash Fruitman, and Lisa Sussman. *Am I Weird or Is This Normal? Advice and Info to Get Teens in the Know* (Fireside, 2001).

Web sites

www.bam.gov

www.girlynation.com

www.kidshealth.org/teen

www.teenadvice.about.com

www.teencentral.net

www.teenmag.com

www.teenvoices.com

www.young-expressions.com

About divorce

www.goaskalice.columbia.edu/1645.html

index

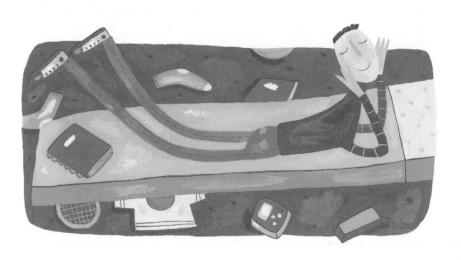